Little RIDDLERS

Cornwall & Devon

Edited By Daisy Job

First published in Great Britain in 2018 by:

Young Writers
Remus House
Coltsfoot Drive
Peterborough
PE2 9BF
Telephone: 01733 890066
Website: www.youngwriters.co.uk

FOREWORD

Dear Reader,

Are you ready to get your thinking caps on to puzzle your way through this wonderful collection?

Young Writers' Little Riddlers competition set out to encourage young writers to create their own riddles. Their answers could be whatever or whoever their imaginations desired; from people to places, animals to objects, food to seasons. Riddles are a great way to further the children's use of poetic expression, including onomatopoeia and similes, as well as encourage them to 'think outside the box' by providing clues without giving the answer away immediately.

All of us here at Young Writers believe in the importance of inspiring young children to produce creative writing, including poetry, and we feel that seeing their own riddles in print will keep that creative spirit burning brightly and proudly.

We hope you enjoy riddling your way through this book as much as we enjoyed reading all the entries.

CONTENTS

Aidan Hughes (5) 52

Ava Cooke (6) 53

Maia Gokhale (5) 54

Emily Harris (6) 55

Edith Coldron (5) 56

Sophia Bellamy (5) 57

Joe Bowden (5) 58

Mount Hawke Academy, Mount Hawke

Henry Colwell (7) 59

Tilda Wesson (6) 60

Carys Sturgeon (7) 61

Esme Pascoe (7) 62

Polly Jarvis (7) 63

Libby Skelton (7) 64

Nicola Gabriela Costa (7) 65

Bryher Elliott (7) 66

Maisie Instance (7) 67

Tassy Ward (7) 68

Kai Deacon (7) 69

Amie Lambert (7) 70

Joseph Thomas Palombo (6) 71

Saria Snell (7) 72

Joshi James (7) 73

Jago Thomas Mattock (6) 74

Mylo Langley (7) 75

Elian Kew-Jones (7) 76

Barnaby Goodright (6) 77

Isaac Brazier (6) 78

Rio Carder (7) 79

Josh Wagg (6) 80

Isabella Marie Rowe (7) 81

Charlie John (6) 82

Nylah Chowney (6) 83

Isla Anne Wilkin (6) 84

Ben Rabey (6) 85

Lowen Noall (6) 86

Maisie Eliot (6) 87

Reuben Henry (5) 88

India Sophia King-Adcock (5) 89

Jack Stephen (6) 90

Charlotte Selley (6) 91

Jessica Cowling (6) 92

St John's International School, Broadway

James Seldon (7) 93

Finn Parker-Larkin (7) 94

Ophelia Cracknell (7) 95

Oscar John Ashford (6) 96

Felix Patmore (7) 97

George Bower (7) 98

Leo Swallow (6) 99

Joel Price (7) 100

Toby Williams (7) 101

Stanley Fudge (6) 102

Emily Pike (6) 103

Kairos De Ville (6) 104

St Petroc's School, Bude

Lucas Tony Chambers (5) 105

Rosie-May Colborne (5) 106

Benjamin Vinciguerra (6) 107

Serena Bray (6) 108

Max Cooper (5) 109

Faith Hesnan (4) 110

Mila Ageneau (5) 111

Isabel Swan (4) 112

Neva-Mae Janse Van Rensburg (5) 113

Noah Clifton-Peters (4) 114

Madelyn Vinciguerra (4) 115

Willow Craxton (4) 116

Tregadillett CP School, Tregadillett

Jack Payne (5) 117

Frankie Skye Goodenough (5) 118

Archie Sanders (6) 119

Olivia Branch (5) 120

Harry Stone (6) 121

Willow Breed (5) 122

Woodfield Primary School, Whitleigh

Amelia Marie Jeffery (7)	123
Tao Cabanga (6)	124
Ruby Dyer (7)	125
Mia Tickle (7)	126
Joshua Llewellyn (7)	127
Lilly Mclelland (6)	128
Rylie Levi Lewendon (6)	129
Layla Drew (6)	130
Charlie Robinson (6)	131
Angel Morris (7)	132
Ollie Kellow (6)	133
Lyla Scannell (7)	134
Tommy Mcelland (6)	135
Eva-May Todd (7)	136
Ava Redgrave (7)	137
Aland Mooney (7)	138
Logan Glibbery (6)	139
Max Bailey (7)	140

THE POEMS

Creepy Me

I have long, fine legs.
I am very large.
I have very sticky feet.
I have sharp fangs.
I'm fuzzy.
I have long, creepy legs.
I have eight legs.
I have sharp, grey, silver wings.
I like biting people.
I crawl very fast.
What am I?

Answer: A tarantula.

Sophie Jane Robson (7)
Delaware Community Primary School, Drakewalls

The Brown Scuttler

I am spiky.
I have eight legs.
I am colourful.
I live in the soil.
I am creepy.
I have white eyes.
I am as small as a mouse.
I am as ugly as a zombie.
I am scary.
I have spiky points.
I always get frightened.
What am I?

Answer: A centipede.

Charlie Samuel Taylor (6)
Delaware Community Primary School, Drakewalls

The Pink Riddle

I have little legs.
I am long.
I am stripy.
I am slimy.
I am scary.
I am stinky.
I am sticky.
I have red eyes.
I have a red body.
I am big.
I am frightening.
What am I?

Answer: A worm.

Maria Carmen Richardson (6)
Delaware Community Primary School, Drakewalls

The Fuzzy Crawler

I have a little shell as my egg.
I eat nice, green leaves for my food.
I have a very fuzzy body.
I eat a lot of leaves.
I go into a cocoon.
I wake up and I am a butterfly.
What am I?

Answer: A caterpillar.

Reggie Gates (7)
Delaware Community Primary School, Drakewalls

Flowers

I have two wings that lift me up to the sky.
I like flowers very much because I eat them.
I have four legs.
I don't bite very much.
I have very sharp teeth.
I look cool.
What am I?

Answer: A busy bee.

Isla Rooke (7)
Delaware Community Primary School, Drakewalls

The Fluffy Hopper

I am as fluffy as a jumper.
I have long ears like a dog.
I am as cute as a cat.
I have claws like a bear.
I hop like you.
You might see me in meadows.
What am I?

Answer: A rabbit.

Kyle O'Donoghue (6)
Delaware Community Primary School, Drakewalls

Fly In The Sky

I have two fast wings.
I have many colours.
I fly in the sky.
I have a tiny, soft body.
I change shape four times.
I have six thin legs
What am I?

Answer: A butterfly.

Seth Alexander Blaze (6)

Delaware Community Primary School, Drakewalls

I Am Hoppy

I have fluffy fur.
I am warm.
I have ten sharp teeth.
I have big eyes.
I am an animal.
I stand on all of my legs.
What am I?

Answer: A rabbit.

Imogen Cook (6)
Delaware Community Primary School, Drakewalls

The Small Orange Beak

I have a big beak
And I am black.
I have blue eyes
And small feet.
I like fish
And I have a white belly.
What am I?

Answer: A penguin.

Michael Healy (7)
Delaware Community Primary School, Drakewalls

The Fluffy Paws

I have black and white fur.
I have claws.
My name is Fluffy.
I have fluffy paws.
I am like a dog.
What am I?

Answer: A cat.

Isabel Dennis (5)
Delaware Community Primary School, Drakewalls

Slowcoach

I am a girl
I am slow.
I don't have any ears.
I want to get into the water.
Sometimes when I go into the water
I get injured.
I have a shiny shell.
I like to swim in the deep water.
I like to swim with my friends and family.
Sometimes I stub my toe
and hurt myself.

Answer: A turtle.

Isla Keeley (6) & Keira Endcott (6)
Ernesettle Community Primary School, Ernesettle

What Am I?

I climb in the trees.
I'm a wild animal.
I can roar very loud.
I'm black and white.
I love eating grass.
I play with toys.
I love the dark.
I see people every day.
I live in the jungle.
I have sharp teeth.
I have red eyes.
What am I?

Answer: A panda.

Lily (6) & Charlotte Elizabeth Burman
Ernesettle Community Primary School, Ernesettle

What Am I?

I am red and green.
I have leaves on me.
I live on the grass.
I am outside.
People work by me.
People sometimes pick me up.
I sometimes live by houses.
I live by the other things on the grass.
What am I?

Answer: A rose.

Nevaeh Dunn (6) & Gracie Russell
Ernesettle Community Primary School, Ernesettle

Yummy Stuff

I am decorated really pretty.
I am given at birthdays.
I have lots of colourful candles.
I am very yummy.
I come in flavours like chocolate,
strawberry and vanilla.
I have lots of icing on me.
What am I?

Answer: A cake.

Ava Mai Edwards (6)
Ernesettle Community Primary School, Ernesettle

Learning Riddles

We listen.
We sit at a desk.
The people have lanyards.
They're sometimes bossy!
They use visualisers.
We wear uniforms.
We have whiteboards
And we have friends.
What is it?

Answer: School.

Jack Rigby (7)
Ernesettle Community Primary School, Ernesettle

Clippy Cloppy

I have hooves that shine.
I have brown fur.
I make a sound, *neigh, neigh.*
My fur is smooth.
I like hay and carrots for food.
I live on a farm in a stable.
What am I?

Answer: A horse.

Heidi Rose Webb (6) & Frankie-Rhian Hoare (7)
Ernesettle Community Primary School, Ernesettle

Famous People From The Past

I am someone from the past.
I am a nurse.
I help soldiers in the war.
I am training nurses.
I am normally called the Lady with the Lamp.
Who am I?

Answer: Florence Nightingale.

Mylee Cotton (6) & Amelia Cotton

Ernesettle Community Primary School, Ernesettle

The Fantastic Riddle

I am juicy.
After you brush your teeth it gets sour.
You need to cut me before eating me.
I am yummy.
You need to pick the top off me.
I am red.
What am I?

Answer: A strawberry.

Faith Gbinoba (7)
Ernesettle Community Primary School, Ernesettle

Ice

I live in the Antarctic.
I eat fish.
I am black and white.
I have an orange nose.
I live somewhere cold.
I come in different shapes and sizes.
What am I?

Answer: A penguin.

Ruby Thornton-Gregory (7) & Adam John Pashby
Ernesettle Community Primary School, Ernesettle

Crunch, Crunch

I have stick arms.
I melt in the sun.
I have a carrot nose.
I am made out of snow.
I can't move.
I am only white.
Who am I?

Answer: Frosty the snowman.

Ryan (6) & Freddie May (6)
Ernesettle Community Primary School, Ernesettle

Back In Time

I eat meat.
My teeth are razor-sharp.
I lived 60 million years ago.
I'm in Jurassic World.
I've taken down something bigger than me.
What am I?

Answer: A T-rex.

Riley Sollick (6)
Ernesettle Community Primary School, Ernesettle

What Am I?

I am yellow.
I am a Pokémon.
I shoot thunderbolts.
My cheeks are chubby
And the colour of fire.
I shoot electricity.
Who am I?

Answer: Pikachu.

Liam (7) & Bravno
Ernesettle Community Primary School, Ernesettle

A Kind Smile At School

They help us learn at school a lot.
They are very kind.
They teach children.
They help us.
They sometimes make me laugh.
What are they?

Answer: Teachers.

Ethan Cotter (7) & Alahna
Ernesettle Community Primary School, Ernesettle

Mushroom Kingdom

I wear a hat.
My favourite food is spaghetti.
I wear gloves.
I have dungarees.
I have a brother.
I have a girlfriend.
Who am I?

Answer: Mario.

Oscar Glynn (6) & Mason Collins (7)
Ernesettle Community Primary School, Ernesettle

What Am I?

I run really fast.
I hunt for food.
I am soft and furry.
I am dangerous to stand near.
I am king of the jungle.
What am I?

Answer: A cheetah.

Mason James David Weldon (6) & Harry

Ernesettle Community Primary School, Ernesettle

What Am I?

I am grey.
My skin is very dry.
I am bigger than a human.
I have big ears.
I have white, pointy tusks.
What am I?

Answer: An elephant.

Thomas Perrin (7)
Ernesettle Community Primary School, Ernesettle

What Am I?

I am grey.
My skin is very dry.
I am bigger than a human.
I have big ears.
And a very long trunk.
What am I?

Answer: An elephant.

Max Osborne (6)
Ernesettle Community Primary School, Ernesettle

Flutter, Flutter

I can fly.
I am symmetrical.
I am like a moth.
I transform from a caterpillar.
I live in the sky.
What am I?

Answer: A butterfly.

Darcie Beavan (7) & Baylee Medway (6)
Ernesettle Community Primary School, Ernesettle

The Fantastic Pet

I have lots of energy.
I am very cute.
I am fluffy.
I do not live in the wild.
I run in a wheel.
What am I?

Answer: A hamster.

Mia Isobel Nancollis (6)
Ernesettle Community Primary School, Ernesettle

What Am I?

I have four paws.
I have black whiskers.
I have a tail.
I have claws to scratch.
I can climb trees.
What am I?

Answer: A cat.

Lillee Walker (6)
Ernesettle Community Primary School, Ernesettle

Power

I am orange, black and sometimes red.
I am furry and fluffy.
I have stripes.
My name starts with a T.
What am I?

Answer: A tiger.

Jaamie Hoskin (7)
Ernesettle Community Primary School, Ernesettle

Feathers

I am skinny.
I can fly.
You can keep me as a pet.
I am thin.
I have feathers.
I also cheep.
What am I?

Answer: A bird.

Georgia Stallard (7)
Ernesettle Community Primary School, Ernesettle

King Of The Ice

I have a fat belly.
I am good.
I am fluffy.
I have red eyes.
I eat fish.
I have feet.
What am I?

Answer: A polar bear.

Ramil Bikovs (6) & Luke Curtis
Ernesettle Community Primary School, Ernesettle

Roar!

I am furry.
I am king of the jungle.
I hunt for prey.
I roam the African wild.
I have a tail.
What am I?

Answer: A tiger.

Jack Peacock (6)
Ernesettle Community Primary School, Ernesettle

Crack, Crack

I have no legs.
I have no fingers.
I have no hair.
You can see me when there is snow.
What am I?

Answer: A snowman.

Ned Reilly (6)

Ernesettle Community Primary School, Ernesettle

Jaws

I am underwater.
I am the biggest in the sea.
I can't be a pet.
I have sharp teeth.
What am I?

Answer: A shark.

Oliver Wadge (6)
Ernesettle Community Primary School, Ernesettle

Animal Rescue

I am helpful.
I look after pets.
I wear a blue uniform.
Cats and dogs can be scared.
Who am I?

Answer: A vet.

Reggie Coombes (6)
Ernesettle Community Primary School, Ernesettle

Flying

I've got long fluffy wings.
I like to fly round and round the corridor.
I love my bird table and food.
I love to eat mice.
I live in a tower, it's full of rooms.
I love to go on fire
And be reborn again.
What am I?

Answer: A phoenix.

Arthur Bailey (6)
Gunnislake Primary School, Gunnislake

Insect

I scurry along the floor.
I have two antennae.
I love to eat wood.
I have two eyes.
I have six legs.
I eat your house.
What am I?

Answer: A termite.

George Grundy (6)
Gunnislake Primary School, Gunnislake

Real Life

I have two ears.
I have two eyes.
I have four legs.
I have one tail.
I have one mouth.
My babies are called puppies.
What am I?

Answer: A dog.

Lenny Cox (6)
Gunnislake Primary School, Gunnislake

Pet

I have two eyes.
I have four legs.
I have one tail.
I have two ears.
My babies are puppies.
I like chewing bones.
What am I?

Answer: A dog.

Faye Harris (6)
Gunnislake Primary School, Gunnislake

A Special Boy

I have two eyes.
I have two legs.
I go to Hogwarts.
I'm in a film.
I have a wand.
I have a scar.
Who am I?

Answer: Harry Potter.

Eli Harvey (6)
Gunnislake Primary School, Gunnislake

Gut Shredder

I like hot, swirly meat,
That can be a tasty treat.
I crush my food to slush, and into mush.
Here I come shaking the earth,
Beneath my crushing feet.
With these feet, I could crush 1,000 seats,
If anyone gets in my way, look out!
Here comes my favourite part, eat that meat.
If you ever meet me you will be sorry,
For in a scurry you will be inside my tummy!
With the guts of a dinosaur tummy
It would be quite funny.
What am I?

Answer: A T-rex.

India Zara Caldwell (6)
Meavy CE Primary School, Meavy

Guts On Fire

I search the skies,
Always in disguise
Waiting for a T-rex to kill.
I swoop down and eat from the top.
I scavenge the ground
Looking for a tasty mound of rotting meat
So then comes my favourite point,
Eat, eat, eat!
I am as big as a tree
So dinosaurs are scared of me.
I eat dead dinos big or small,
I just love it all.
What am I?

Answer: A Quetzalcoatlus.

Emmeline Hall (7)
Meavy CE Primary School, Meavy

Scary Snap

Here I come travelling smoothly
Through the bashing, crashing sea.
A juicy fish, a tasty squid
But still not enough food for me.
I see above the ocean with my tall, thin neck
On the look-out for smaller swimming dinos
to wreck.
My short flippers are to smack my prey,
Then here comes my favourite part, play,
play, play.
What am I?

Answer: A Futabasaurus.

Aoife Scawn (7)
Meavy CE Primary School, Meavy

The Great Sea Monster

Me and my family gliding through
the huge ocean as I snatch my prey.
But I go by warning
my family to try to go away.
Then we start a hard fight
to snatch, glide and bite.
But then I won the annoying fight
and I took a big bite.
Then we go home to take a big bite.
I have big sharp teeth and claws to snatch.
What am I?

Answer: A liopleurodon.

Bella Reyburn (7)
Meavy CE Primary School, Meavy

King Of The Deadly Sea Creatures

I am as long as a swimming pool.
You can't fool me, you fools.
Here I come, speeding through the sea
Catching fat fish to eat for tea.
I am a deadly sea creature.
You would never want to mess with me.
Here I come, chasing silly, crazy fish
Who will never, never learn
Because I can catch them.
What am I?

Answer: A liopleurodon.

Noah Dorey (6)
Meavy CE Primary School, Meavy

The Squid Catcher

Fresh squid is my favourite dinner.
When catching food I am always the winner.
I try to keep them gliding through the sea
And fill myself up easily.
I have sharp teeth to snap my prey
And flippers to help me turn away.
My pointy teeth help me to grip
So that the slimy squid don't slip.
What am I?

Answer: A dolichorhynchops.

Grace Gokhale (7)
Meavy CE Primary School, Meavy

Monster Of The Sky

Here I come flying through the air
Trying to find my yummy tea,
In the woodland through the tree.
With my giant beak, I rip and tear
The rotting flesh dead dinos wear.
I leave deep tracks along the way
And take to the sky at the end of the day.
I'm the biggest pterosaur.
What am I?

Answer: A Quetzalcoatlus.

Laila-Mae Thompson (7)

Meavy CE Primary School, Meavy

King Of The Sky

I like to swoop down to the sea
to catch juicy fish.
Here I come swooping along the air
with my sharp beak.
Here I come again with my bigger wings
and my sharper beak.
I am as big as a chicken
and I come out every day.
Here I come swooping for fish.
What am I?

Answer: A rhamphorhynchus.

Alex McAulay Weemys (6)
Meavy CE Primary School, Meavy

The Queen Of The Sea

Fresh fish is my favourite thing to eat.
I munch my food whilst I swim for a treat.
My family and I search the water for some food.
My family and I travel around the world for some food for our tea.
We saw a kronosaurus, he caught us
But then we were free.
What am I?

Answer: A futabasaurus.

Lucy Hulbert (7)

Meavy CE Primary School, Meavy

Bone Cruncher

I am the biggest meat-eater in the world.
Here I come stamping
through the hard ground
Waiting for a triceratops
or a really tasty tree.
I am on the look-out for danger.
I have sharp teeth.
My colour is silver.
My favourite food is meat.
What am I?

Answer: A Giganotosaurus.

Aidan Hughes (5)
Meavy CE Primary School, Meavy

Fish Beware

Here I come gliding through the wide ocean,
Chasing fish and causing a commotion.
My thin flippers help me turn,
The silly fish won't ever learn.
With dagger-like teeth I snatch up squid
From out of places where they hid.
What am I?

Answer: A dolichorhynchops.

Ava Cooke (6)
Meavy CE Primary School, Meavy

Plant Muncher

I have a short tail.
I have a comb on my head.
I have two short arms
And two long legs.
I walk on two legs.
I have a curvy back.
I can run as fast as a giraffe.
I eat leaves, plants and flowers
And they are yummy.
What am I?

Answer: A lambeosaurus.

Maia Gokhale (5)
Meavy CE Primary School, Meavy

Guts And Blood Of Dinosaurs

I prowl around the dinosaur land.
I eat fat meat,
It is a treat every day.
I have a mighty jaw.
I eat everyone I see.
When I see another dinosaur
I rip it apart
Before it knows I am about in one gulp.
What am I?

Answer: A T-rex.

Emily Harris (6)
Meavy CE Primary School, Meavy

Friendly Plant Eater

I have a comb on my head.
I stand on two legs.
I am as fast as a giraffe.
Nose to tail I am 55 feet.
I am as heavy as five black rhinos.
My name begins with L.
What am I?

Answer: A lambeosaurus.

Edith Coldron (5)
Meavy CE Primary School, Meavy

Charging, Vegging

I like eating plants.
When I munch I look out for danger.
With my horns, I charge at any dinos
that try to eat me.
All day long I eat juicy leaves.
What am I?

Answer: A styracosaurus.

Sophia Bellamy (5)
Meavy CE Primary School, Meavy

Boy Monster

Look out, I might kill you
With my pointy teeth.
I stomp through bogs
and rivers to catch fish.
I am a carnivore.
I have a big fan on my back.
What am I?

Answer: A spinosaurus.

Joe Bowden (5)
Meavy CE Primary School, Meavy

Rainforest Riddle

I live in South America.
I have toes as orange as lava.
I sleep protected in leaves.
I like to climb trees
with my suction cups on my toes.
I have eyes as red as blood
streaming out of your hand.
I am very rarely found hiding behind trees.
I like to jump high on to branches.
I live in the rainforest by lakes.
I eat insects, crickets
and other smaller frogs.
I have a chest as grey as a rock.
I can grow up to 2cm long.
I am as green as a leaf.
What am I?

Answer: A red-eyed tree frog.

Henry Colwell (7)
Mount Hawke Academy, Mount Hawke

My Rainforest Riddle

I have very sticky feet and red eyes.
I eat beetles, crickets and bugs.
I really like swimming in the beautiful,
swampy lake.
I live in the wet, green leaves.
I am green and sticky
and have a long tongue like a snake.
I have orange feet
and I can have babies.
I can climb up big wet trees.
I am as green as a light green leaf.
I live in South America mostly.
I can lay eggs
and protect them from predators.
I am very small so I can hide very well.
What am I?

Answer: A tree frog.

Tilda Wesson (6)
Mount Hawke Academy, Mount Hawke

Rainforest Riddle

I live in the rainforest.
I am colourful.
I can live up to 12 years old.
I live in East Africa, North Mozambique
and Tanzania.
I eat small juicy animals such as little birds
and tiny insects.
I like to sunbathe.
I grow up to 70cm long.
I change colours and patterns
to match my emotions and feelings.
I sunbathe in the blazing tropic sun
That is as hot as a sauna.
What am I?

Answer: A chameleon.

Carys Sturgeon (7)
Mount Hawke Academy, Mount Hawke

Rainforest Riddle

I eat insects and I am a carnivore.
I live in the tropical rainforest.
My body grows up to 7cm long.
My weight is 14.4oz (408g).
My normal appearance is deep green
with peculiar black spots
and also yellow stripes.
I live in the east of Africa
and I climb on trees.
I change colour to tell how I am feeling.
I am as green as grass.
What am I?

Answer: A chameleon.

Esme Pascoe (7)
Mount Hawke Academy, Mount Hawke

Rainforest Riddle

I live in a big, messy nest
and I am over the top with seeds and nuts.
I love my big, strong, tough, thick
and bony wings.
I can grow very big, about a metre long.
I have a bone in my tongue
and I like to use it like a tool.
I do like to use my wings
so I get pretty strong.
I like to sit on a branch
when I am feeding my babies.
What am I?

Answer: A macaw.

Polly Jarvis (7)
Mount Hawke Academy, Mount Hawke

Rainforest Riddle

I live in the rainforest.
I am 30cm to 100cm long.
I am an omnivore
and some of my friends eat damp soil.
I like to fly in a flock.
I can also mimic human speech.
I have a red body like blood.
I have green and blue wings
as blue as the sea
and a yellow beak.
What am I?

Answer: A macaw.

Libby Skelton (7)
Mount Hawke Academy, Mount Hawke

Rainforest Riddle

I fly up in the canopy.
I am an intelligent, social bird
That often gathers in flocks of 10 to 30.
I have colourful feathers as colourful as a
rainbow.
I like to eat fruit, nuts, insects and snails.
I live in the rainforest in the canopy.
I am very colourful.
What am I?

Answer: A macaw.

Nicola Gabriela Costa (7)
Mount Hawke Academy, Mount Hawke

Rainforest Riddle

I eat leaves and live in the rainforest.
I love cecropia trees, it is my favourite.
I weigh 8-9 pounds.
I have a short snout.
I am as slow as a snail.
I am the slowest thing on Earth.
I have long claws.
I live in the trees.
I am brown.
What am I?

Answer: A sloth.

Bryher Elliott (7)
Mount Hawke Academy, Mount Hawke

Rainforest Riddle

I live in the rainforest.
I have a curly tail.
I am green all over me.
I am camouflaged.
I have stripes on me.
I am small.
I have black eyes.
I can grow up to 70cm long.
I can live as long as 12 years.
I have black spots.
What am I?

Answer: A chameleon.

Maisie Instance (7)
Mount Hawke Academy, Mount Hawke

Rainforest Riddle

I live in the rainforest.
I eat twigs, leaves and fruit.
I spend most of my time in trees.
I only come down once a week!
I have sharp claws and teeth.
I love to climb.
I am as slow as a snail.
I am brown and furry.
I have a snout.
What am I?

Answer: A sloth.

Tassy Ward (7)
Mount Hawke Academy, Mount Hawke

Rainforest Riddle

I have a 19cm bill which attracts a mate.
I have a black strap around my bill.
I like to fly around the canopy of South America.
I use my bill as a weapon.
I love to eat birds' eggs and lizards.
I live in a small flock of about six birds.
What am I?

Answer: A toucan.

Kai Deacon (7)
Mount Hawke Academy, Mount Hawke

Rainforest Riddle

I live in the tropical forests
of Central and South America.
You will find me upside down in trees.
My fur is brown and fluffy.
I eat leaves, twigs and fruit.
I only go down to the ground once a week.
I like to sleep and I am very slow.
What am I?

Answer: A sloth.

Amie Lambert (7)
Mount Hawke Academy, Mount Hawke

Rainforest Riddle

I live to five years old.
I like to jump on leaves.
I don't like being dirty.
I like to go in water.
I like to climb trees.
I am 2cm but males can grow to 3-4cm.
I have red eyes.
I eat crickets mostly.
What am I?

Answer: A red-eyed tree frog.

Joseph Thomas Palombo (6)
Mount Hawke Academy, Mount Hawke

Rainforest Riddle

I am a carnivore
And mostly I eat insects.
I live near water, rivers
And streams in South America.
My eyes are as red as red paint.
I live in the lowland.
I have a long tongue.
I have suction cups on my toes.
What am I?

Answer: A red-eyed tree frog.

Saria Snell (7)
Mount Hawke Academy, Mount Hawke

Rainforest Riddle

I live in East Africa.
I like to sunbathe.
I weigh up to 408g
and grow to 50cm.
I also live up to 12 years.
I look like a small leaf and am very green.
I eat insects and small birds.
What am I?

Answer: A chameleon.

Joshi James (7)
Mount Hawke Academy, Mount Hawke

Rainforest Riddle

I am as green as a leaf.
I live in South America.
I live next to rivers and streams.
I hide my colours at night.
I eat frogs and crickets.
Boys are 2cms and girls are 3cms.
What am I?

Answer: A red-eyed tree frog.

Jago Thomas Mattock (6)
Mount Hawke Academy, Mount Hawke

Rainforest Riddle

I am a carnivore.
I am 70cm long, as long as a snake.
I live in the Amazon rainforest.
I live up to 12 years.
I eat insects and small birds.
I change colour patterns.
What am I?

Answer: A chameleon.

Mylo Langley (7)
Mount Hawke Academy, Mount Hawke

Rainforest Riddle

I eat fruit, nuts, snails, insects
And damp soil.
I am as screechy as a seagull.
I like to fly.
I live in the canopy.
I grow up to 100cm long.
I am multicoloured.
What am I?

Answer: A macaw.

Elian Kew-Jones (7)
Mount Hawke Academy, Mount Hawke

My Rainforest Riddle

I live in a tree.
I may be scary.
I have a sticky tummy
that I rub on a tree to warn off enemies.
I hate to be called a bear.
I carry my young in a pouch.
What am I?

Answer: A koala.

Barnaby Goodright (6)
Mount Hawke Academy, Mount Hawke

Rainforest Riddle

I live in the rainforest trees.
My wingspan is 127cm.
I gather in flocks from 10 to 30.
I love flying.
I eat nuts and seeds as hard as wood.
I am a bird.
What am I?

Answer: A macaw.

Isaac Brazier (6)

Mount Hawke Academy, Mount Hawke

My Rainforest Riddle

I'm as green as a leaf.
I live in South America.
I eat insects.
I have a small body.
I lay eggs.
I like climbing trees
And I like swimming.
What am I?

Answer: A tree frog.

Rio Carder (7)

Mount Hawke Academy, Mount Hawke

My Rainforest Riddle

I am one of the smallest animals
In the rainforest.
Do not touch me, I am poisonous.
I am as small as a spider.
I am clever.
I eat bugs.
What am I?

Answer: A poison dart frog.

Josh Wagg (6)
Mount Hawke Academy, Mount Hawke

Rainforest Riddle

I live in South America.
I have a yellow beak.
I have black eyes.
I eat bugs and insects.
I like tropical trees.
I am a carnivore.
What am I?

Answer: A toucan.

Isabella Marie Rowe (7)
Mount Hawke Academy, Mount Hawke

My Rainforest Riddle

I am poisonous.
I live in wet leaves.
I am brightly coloured.
I scare away other animals.
You will be scared to touch me.
What am I?

Answer: A dart frog.

Charlie John (6)
Mount Hawke Academy, Mount Hawke

My Rainforest Riddle

I fly up in the sky.
I'm rainbow coloured.
I have sharp claws.
I have a pointy beak.
I'm really good at flying.
What am I?

Answer: A parrot.

Nylah Chowney (6)
Mount Hawke Academy, Mount Hawke

My Rainforest Riddle

I squeeze my prey.
I eat them whole.
I am long.
I am as scary as a tiger.
I have lots of venom inside of me.
What am I?

Answer: A tree snake.

Isla Anne Wilkin (6)

Mount Hawke Academy, Mount Hawke

My Rainforest Riddle

I live on grassy mountains.
I like to climb trees.
I live in China.
I eat bamboo.
I am black and white.
What am I?

Answer: A panda.

Ben Rabey (6)
Mount Hawke Academy, Mount Hawke

My Rainforest Riddle

I live in a rainforest.
I look hairy.
I like bananas.
I am orange like fire.
I have long arms.
What am I?

Answer: An orangutan.

Lowen Noall (6)
Mount Hawke Academy, Mount Hawke

My Rainforest Riddle

I have brown fur.
I live in the rainforest.
I use my claws to hang in trees.
I eat leaves and fruit.
What am I?

Answer: A sloth.

Maisie Eliot (6)

Mount Hawke Academy, Mount Hawke

My Rainforest

I am slow like a tortoise
But I cannot swim or fly.
I can climb trees.
I eat plants.
What am I?

Answer: A sloth.

Reuben Henry (5)
Mount Hawke Academy, Mount Hawke

What Am I?

I have a very good sense of smell.
I have stripy fur.
Yes, you know I have eyes.
What am I?

Answer: A magical tiger.

India Sophia King-Adcock (5)
Mount Hawke Academy, Mount Hawke

My Rainforest Riddle

I'm cute like a sloth.
I eat bananas.
I am cheeky.
I screech.
I swing.
What am I?

Answer: A monkey.

Jack Stephen (6)
Mount Hawke Academy, Mount Hawke

My Rainforest Riddle

I live in a tree.
I am lovely and brown.
I like hanging upside down.
What am I?

Answer: A sloth.

Charlotte Selley (6)
Mount Hawke Academy, Mount Hawke

What Am I?

I am furry.
I eat carrots.
I live in a field.
What am I?

Answer: A rabbit.

Jessica Cowling (6)
Mount Hawke Academy, Mount Hawke

Sparkly Silver

My colour is silver.
I'm used for wrapping.
You can find me in the supermarket.
You put me on a Christmas tree.
I am sparkly.
I only come out at Christmas.
What am I?

Answer: Tinsel.

James Seldon (7)
St John's International School, Broadway

Tree Stomper

I am big.
You can climb in me.
You can find cool stuff in me.
You can get lost in me.
There are lots of trees here.
People walk through me.
What am I?

Answer: A wood.

Finn Parker-Larkin (7)
St John's International School, Broadway

The Rabbit Lover

I am a burnt orange.
I have a swishy tail.
I like to eat chickens and rabbits.
I live in a den.
My predator is a lynx.
I have sharp teeth.
What am I?

Answer: A fox.

Ophelia Cracknell (7)
St John's International School, Broadway

Fluffy Cat

I am really fast.
I leap out of the bushes for my predators.
I am not calm.
I have sharp teeth.
I have spots on my fur.
I eat meat.
What am I?

Answer: A cheetah.

Oscar John Ashford (6)
St John's International School, Broadway

Slitherer

I am long and big.
I slither on the grass.
I am light green.
I eat mice.
I've got a pointy tongue.
I have an orange eye.
What am I?

Answer: A snake.

Felix Patmore (7)
St John's International School, Broadway

Big And Tasty

I am soft meat.
I have a fluffy bun.
People eat me.
I come with soft chips.
I am yummy
and I come with delicious ketchup.
What am I?

Answer: A burger.

George Bower (7)
St John's International School, Broadway

Living Robot

I have a nose.

I have a big eye and a small eye.

I have toes.

I have a neck.

I have eyebrows.

I have eyelashes.

What am I?

Answer: A person.

Leo Swallow (6)

St John's International School, Broadway

The Predator

I have silky fur.
My predator is a bison.
I eat meat.
I am scary.
I live in the forest.
I have sharp teeth.
What am I?

Answer: A wolf.

Joel Price (7)
St John's International School, Broadway

The Noise Maker

I fly like a bird.
I have points on my wings.
I am noisy.
I have glass windows.
I carry people.
I am big.
What am I?

Answer: A plane.

Toby Williams (7)
St John's International School, Broadway

Scary Beast

I am big.
I like swimming.
I have teeth.
I have a long tail.
I have scales.
I live on land or water.
What am I?

Answer: A crocodile.

Stanley Fudge (6)
St John's International School, Broadway

Cries

I am small.
I am cheeky.
I am living.
I wear clothes.
I have two milk teeth.
I drink milk.
What am I?

Answer: A baby.

Emily Pike (6)
St John's International School, Broadway

Striper

I am fast.
I am scary.
I have sharp teeth.
I am big.
I eat meat.
I am a type of cat.
What am I?

Answer: A tiger.

Kairos De Ville (6)
St John's International School, Broadway

A Fluffy Friend

I can climb trees.
I eat eucalyptus plants.
I have a pouch to carry my babies.
I have big fluffy ears.
I look cuddly but I have sharp claws.
I live in Australia.
What am I?

Answer: A koala bear.

Lucas Tony Chambers (5)
St Petroc's School, Bude

A Man's Best Small Friend

I sleep a lot.
I like a nice soft bed.
I like to chew smelly socks.
I might miss my mummy.
I like lots of toys to play with.
I am very soft and very lovable.
What am I?

Answer: A puppy.

Rosie-May Colborne (5)
St Petroc's School, Bude

Go Quackers

I can swim in rivers.
I can waddle down the riverside.
I have two webbed feet.
I have a sharp beak.
My babies follow me.
I say quack.
What am I?

Answer: A duck.

Benjamin Vinciguerra (6)
St Petroc's School, Bude

The Baby Slitherer

I live in the jungle.
I am long and thin.
I like a juicy mouse to eat.
I have a rattle tail.
I move very sssslowly.
What am I?

Answer: A rattlesnake.

Serena Bray (6)
St Petroc's School, Bude

Machine Menace

I am made of metal.
I live in a house.
I like to be built.
I have controls.
I can talk.
I am hard.
What am I?

Answer: A robot.

Max Cooper (5)
St Petroc's School, Bude

Royal Jewels

I am golden.
I have diamonds on me.
I go on someone's head.
A queen wears me.
I live in a castle.
What am I?

Answer: A crown.

Faith Hesnan (4)
St Petroc's School, Bude

Sky Flyer

I have a horn.
I am an animal.
I have wings.
I like to fly in the sky.
I am pink.
What am I?

Answer: A unicorn.

Mila Ageneau (5)
St Petroc's School, Bude

Icy Queen

I wear blue.
I have a snowflake.
I like to sing 'Let It Go'.
My sister is Anna.
Who am I?

Answer: Elsa.

Isabel Swan (4)
St Petroc's School, Bude

Fluffy Friend

I eat carrots.
I am white.
I live underground.
I jump.
I have long ears.
What am I?

Answer: A rabbit.

Neva-Mae Janse Van Rensburg (5)
St Petroc's School, Bude

Purple Wheels

I am purple.
I have four wheels.
I go *brum*.
What am I?

Answer: Mummy's car.

Noah Clifton-Peters (4)
St Petroc's School, Bude

No Clothes On Me!

I have wings.
I eat carrots.
I have a horn.
I am naked.
What am I?

Answer: A unicorn.

Madelyn Vinciguerra (4)
St Petroc's School, Bude

I Come In The Night

I have wings.
I am little.
I collect teeth.
Who am I?

Answer: The Tooth Fairy.

Willow Craxton (4)

St Petroc's School, Bude

Emma Jade

I drive on all 12 wheels
Going strong past the fields.
Uphill, downhill and round the bend,
but be careful!
I'm very long.
I go for miles and miles,
and on my back, you will find lots of styles.
All us girls in a fleet,
carrying the driver in his seat.
What am I?

Answer: An Eddie Stobart lorry.

Jack Payne (5)
Tregadillett CP School, Tregadillett

Bounce, Bounce, Bounce

I have a brown fur coat
with long, beautiful ears.
I love eating carrots for my lunch.
I like to eat bananas
and nibble all my food.
Cats might sneak up on me
and catch me for their tea.
I like to bounce and hop around
Then cuddle up with my favourite friend.
What am I?

Answer: A rabbit.

Frankie Skye Goodenough (5)
Tregadillett CP School, Tregadillett

Archie's Red Riddle

I am a very juicy, red fruit.
If I am not ripe, I stay green.
I am very sweet to eat.
I grow best in the heat.
I am often used in a smoothie.
I am made into jam and jellies.
You can go into a field
and pick me in your wellies.
What am I?

Answer: A strawberry.

Archie Sanders (6)
Tregadillett CP School, Tregadillett

Flock

Some of us are small,
Some of us are big.
Some of us can swim
but not all of us can fly.
Some of us can chirp,
Some of us can squawk.
Some have long legs,
Some have short,
but we all have a beak.
What are we?

Answer: Birds.

Olivia Branch (5)
Tregadillett CP School, Tregadillett

Meat Eater

I have three claws on one hand.
I am the biggest to roam the land.
I have razor-sharp teeth.
I think I am the chief.
I can roar really loud,
so loud it can reach the clouds.
What am I?

Answer: A spinosaurus.

Harry Stone (6)
Tregadillett CP School, Tregadillett

What Am I?

I have a long neck.
I have brown and yellow colours.
I love to eat leaves.
I have a long tongue.
I live in Africa.
I am the world's tallest animal.
What am I?

Answer: A giraffe.

Willow Breed (5)
Tregadillett CP School, Tregadillett

Shiny Gold

I belong to the richest pirate.
I am sometimes found in a wooden chest.
I am very shiny and pretty like the sun.
I can be found under the sea or ground.
I can be stolen by other pirates.
I can be found by a dirty old map.
What am I?

Answer: Treasure.

Amelia Marie Jeffery (7)
Woodfield Primary School, Whitleigh

What Am I?

I have been worn by awesome, scary
pirates.
I am brown like a beautiful, hard tree.
I might be on weak, silver boots.
I am like a hard, tough tree.
I get used for injured pirates.
I get worn on bony, bleeding legs.
What am I?

Answer: A wooden leg.

Tao Cabanga (6)
Woodfield Primary School, Whitleigh

Bad Enemies

I shot my best friend in the knee.
I have four lovely wives.
I have a horrible hairy crew.
I am the best pirate.
I have Queen Anne's Revenge ship.
I have nice treasure,
It followed me when I died.
Who am I?

Answer: Blackbeard.

Ruby Dyer (7)
Woodfield Primary School, Whitleigh

The Bright Ocean

I have yellow sand.
I have treasure everywhere.
I have tall trees everywhere.
I have sparkly water around me.
I have treasure hidden.
I have crews walking on me.
What am I?

Answer: Treasure Island.

Mia Tickle (7)
Woodfield Primary School, Whitleigh

Ahoy!

I am really rusty.
I help with awesome ships.
I have a point on each side.
I am used most of the time.
I can't be lifted by a person.
I am very, very, very heavy.
What am I?

Answer: An anchor.

Joshua Llewellyn (7)
Woodfield Primary School, Whitleigh

Colourful Wings

I have a yellow beak.
I have red and yellow wings.
I have a sharp beak.
I sit on the captain's shoulders.
I fly over the captain's black ship,
The Black Pearl.
What am I?

Answer: A parrot.

Lilly Mclelland (6)
Woodfield Primary School, Whitleigh

Colourful Rainbow

I am bright yellow, orange and red.
I can fly above the fluffy clouds.
I have loads of bright colours.
I have a black hat.
I have a brown beak.
I have orange feet.
What am I?

Answer: A parrot.

Rylie Levi Lewendon (6)
Woodfield Primary School, Whitleigh

Colourful Pirate

I have colourful wings.
I have a black eyepatch.
I have a brown and green face.
I have a zigzag body.
I have two crazy feet.
I sometimes sit on a pirate's arm.
What am I?

Answer: A parrot.

Layla Drew (6)
Woodfield Primary School, Whitleigh

Splish, Splosh

I am used to stop a ship.
I am black.
I am shiny in the water.
I fall to the bottom of the ocean.
I am used to stop a ship to fight.
I am heavy.
I am sharp.
What am I?

Answer: An anchor.

Charlie Robinson (6)
Woodfield Primary School, Whitleigh

Wavy Black Flag

I have black around me.
I am a flag.
I am scary.
I show people that there is a pirate.
My colour is white.
I have two lines under my head.
What am I?

Answer: The Jolly Roger.

Angel Morris (7)
Woodfield Primary School, Whitleigh

Bright Island

I have sand on me.
I have water around me.
I have trees on me.
Sometimes people come to me.
I can't move.
I have got treasure on me.
What am I?

Answer: *Treasure Island.*

Ollie Kellow (6)
Woodfield Primary School, Whitleigh

Fluffy Feathers

I am as colourful as a rainbow.
I can fly like an eagle.
I have two amazing legs.
I have a red, awesome tail.
I help a pirate.
I am fluffy.
What am I?

Answer: A parrot.

Lyla Scannell (7)
Woodfield Primary School, Whitleigh

Ahoy!

I have a skull and crossbones.
I flap like a bird or an eagle.
People look under me.
I am a black flag.
I fly on a pirate ship.
What am I?

Answer: The Jolly Roger.

Tommy Mcelland (6)
Woodfield Primary School, Whitleigh

Huge Serpent

I am huge.
I carry people.
I have a plank.
I sail the seas.
I have a pearl on my sail.
I have lots of shelter on my deck.
What am I?

Answer: A pirate ship.

Eva-May Todd (7)
Woodfield Primary School, Whitleigh

Who Am I?

I have a blunderbuss.
I have a cutlass.
I kill other pirates.
I am a scary lady.
I sail on a ship.
I search for treasure.
Who am I?

Answer: Anne Bonny.

Ava Redgrave (7)
Woodfield Primary School, Whitleigh

The Seven Seas

I am hard and silver.
I have got two sharp points.
I have got two sharp pins.
I am heavier than a person.
I reach the sand.
What am I?

Answer: An anchor.

Aland Mooney (7)
Woodfield Primary School, Whitleigh

Super Sailor

I have a shiny cutlass.
I have a good knife.
I have a nice pistol.
I sail the seven seas.
I sail for the treasure chest.
What am I?

Answer: A pirate.

Logan Glibbery (6)
Woodfield Primary School, Whitleigh

A Colourful Flyer

I am beautiful and cute.
I have green feathers.
I sit on the captain's shoulders.
I have two feet
And a sharp beak.
What am I?

Answer: A parrot.

Max Bailey (7)
Woodfield Primary School, Whitleigh